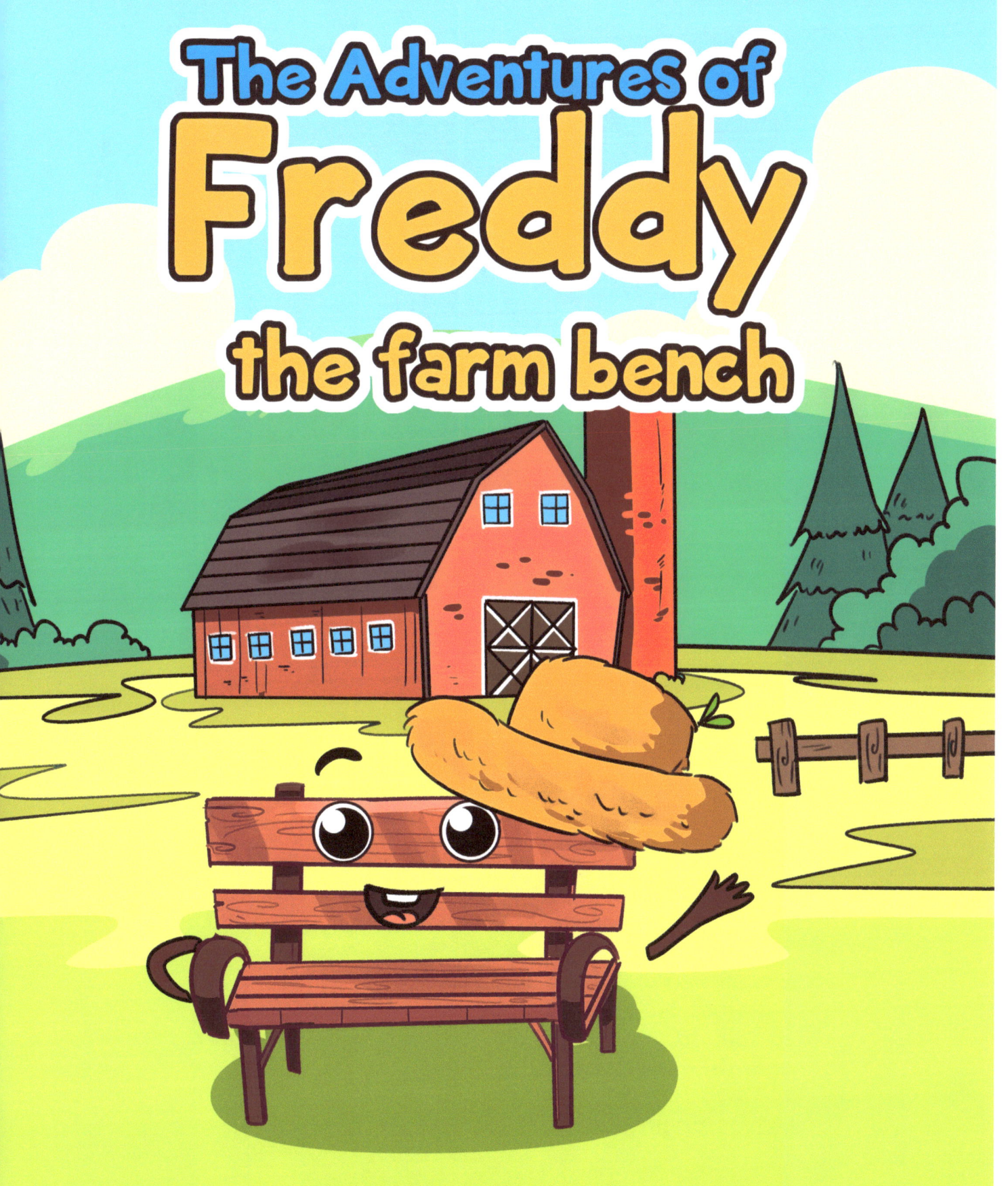

Hi, I am Freddy the farm bench.
Come join me on an adventure through a farm.

I wonder what we will see...
I am not sure, but I know we will be able
to talk to our family and friends about life on a farm
and all the wonderful animals.

Let us begin our farm experience.

Have you ever wondered what it would be like to live on a farm?

It is lots of fun but also lots of work.
No matter what needs to get done, it is a family affair.

Farmers begin their day very early in the morning and end their day very late at night.

Let's look at the life of one farmer and his family. They also have a collie and his name is "Cody".

In the morning, the crow of a rooster wakes everyone up.

"Cock-a-doodle-doooooo!....Cock-a-doodle-doooooo!..."

Roosters are adult male chickens.
They crow to show other roosters it is their territory.

Did you know that roosters can crow in the morning, afternoon or in the evening?

Once the farmer is up, he feeds the cows and calves.

He begins milking the cows very early in the morning.
He also cleans their sheds.
This is all done before the sun rises.

"Moooo!……Moooo!……Moooo!…."

Did you know that cows also bellow, snort and grunt?

The farmer is now ready to prepare all the equipment, tools and material.

He will need his tractor, harvester, ATV, sprayer, plow, fertilizer spreader, wagons and other tools.

His dog is also ready to help.

Farm animals are intelligent, social and depend on farmers for food, shelter and care.

Let's take a look at the most common farm animals.

"Oink!....Oink!.....Oink!....!" Pigs.....pigs.....pigs....

These farm pigs are raised on a diet of feed, fruits and vegetables.

Pigs can be pink, red, black, white or spotted.

What's your favorite pig color?

"Cluck!.....Cluck!....Cluck!..."

I see many chickens.
A chicken can be male or female.

A hen is a female chicken. Hens lay eggs.

After they lay eggs, they make cackling noises.

"Cackle!....Cackle!....Cackle!..."

Oh, look! The eggs are hatching!

Chicks, chicks, chicks.... Chicks are everywhere!

"Cheep!....Cheep!....Cheep!..."

The farmer has to make sure the chicks always have clean water and remember to feed them every day.

Let's go to the pastures.
Pastures are where animals graze.

What animals do you think we will see?

Look at all the sheep!

"Baa!...Baa!...Baa!..."

Female sheep are called ewes and males are called rams.

Young sheep are called lambs.

Sheep graze in the fields,
but they also eat hay and grains.
Some sheep have horns.
They also have thick hair called wool.
Wool can be different colors.
Many things are made from wool.

clothes...socks...hats...scarves...gloves...pillows....
purses...blankets...and more

If you have a favorite sweater, you can thank a sheep.

I see goats! They sound just like sheep.

"Baa!...Baa!...Baa!..."

Female goats are called a doe or nanny.
Male goats are called a buck or billy.
Young goats are called kids.

Goats eat grass, herbs, tree leaves and other plants.
They have horns that grow upwards and backwards.
They can also climb and hold their balance.

If a small kid pushes against you, never push back!

"Neigh!....Neigh!....Neigh!..."

Look at all the horses.
Horses live in herds and are very beautiful.
They can walk, trot, jump and gallop.

Horses are called foals when they are born.
Between one and two years old, they are called yearlings.
If they are younger than four years old,
they are called a colt or a filly.
When they are older than four years old,
they are stallions or mares.

Did you know there are over 350 breeds of horses?

Here are some donkeys and mules.

A female donkey is called Jenny.
A female mule is called Molly.

A male donkey is called Jack.
A male mule can be called Jack or John.

"Burro" is Spanish for donkey.

"EE-Aw-EE-Aw!....EE-Aw-EE-Aw!..."

They are coming to greet us.

A donkey is heavy, but a mule is heavier,
taller and larger than donkeys.
A donkey can reproduce, but a mule can not.
They both can be black, grey or white.

Can you tell the difference between a donkey and a mule?

Let's see other animals that live on this farm.

I see ducks. Do you see ducks?

I see geese. Do you see geese?

I see rabbits. Do you see rabbits?

I see turkeys. Do you see turkeys?

This farmer also grows some fruits and vegetables.

Ready!...Let's take a look!

Wow....He grows apples, berries and melons.....They look delicious!

Can you name other types of fruits farmers grow?

He also grows corn and carrots.

Yummy! Yummy! Yummy!

Can you name other types of vegetables farmers grow?

Well, it's getting late....

The farmer and his family are ready to call it a day.
They have worked very hard....
They need to get a good nights sleep because they will have to do this all over again tomorrow....

We must always "Thank a Farmer" for all they do.

I hope you loved our farm experience.

If you are ready for another adventure,
look for my friend Hercules.
He will introduce you to people that are brave
and courageous.

Hercules will show you heroes from A-Z.
A hero can be male or female…..young or old….

You are going to be surprised to see the heroes
all around you.

Bye, bye….

www.ingramcontent.com/pod-product-compliance
Lightning Source LLC
Chambersburg PA
CBHW041709160426
43209CB00017B/1783